G000150632

BETWE
NOW
AND
THEN

As told by Genie Poretzky-Lee

In memory of Xavier Poretzky 1937–2017

A Blue Lotus Publication 2020

www.genieporetzky-lee.com

First published in 2020 by Blue Lotus Publications

The right of Genie Poretzky-Lee to be identified as the Author of the
Work has been asserted by her in accordance with the Copyright,
Designs and Patents Act 1988.

ISBN: 978-0-99347184-1

With thanks to Anna Walker, Ph.D. for design and layout along with the
sympathetic handling of all images

05. 08. 2021

Dear Salika

Honey in the heart!

In friendship

Gene

'What has been done in time must be
undone with time.'

Colette Aboulker-Muscat

INTRODUCTION

What makes or starts a story? Maybe curiosity, or mostly singular awareness unfolding into different patterns for each of us humans on Earth.

This one, about to be told, is witnessed by siblings, partly as a tale of survival, but equally one of childhood magic experienced in occupied France during the Second World War.

Having now reached a reasonably advanced age, I am giving voice to our childhood with a sense of urgency.

The time has come to awaken the dormant scared child within us and ask for its help in retracing events and feelings hidden between the many-layered depths of time, giving it an opportunity to ring its unique note, and not allowing it to vanish into silent oblivion through careless neglect, without ever reaching the eyes and ears of the next generation.

The memories about to be addressed are not unique. Many children of our generation have an intricate tale to share. The same applies to all war-zone kids these days. Maybe it is important to trace our personal memories for the sake of all children lost in an adult world not of their making or choosing, for which, unknowingly, they may feel a liability, evolving later into unending trauma.

1

Sur la route de Louviers,
Sur la route de Louviers,
Il y avait un cantonnier,
Il y avait un cantonnier,
Et qui cassait,
Et qui cassait,
Des tas d' cailloux,
Des tas d' cailloux,
Et qui cassait des tas d' cailloux
Pour mettre sur l' passag' des roues.

HEARSAY

1934. Born to Grounia Tikotsky and Joseph Poretzky, timber merchant, a daughter named Evgenia (Eugenie), followed three years later by that of a son, Saveli-Xavier, named after his maternal grandfather.

Their parents, fleeing from the Russian revolution, came to settle in the Hanseatic Free City of Danzig, now known as Gdańsk, Poland. Joseph Poretzky's timber business flourished in this commercial port on the shore of the Baltic sea. The family had a prosperous lifestyle; nanny, cook, expensive furnishings and clothing.

Little did they know that their new home's historical abnormality would open a chasm for the German invasion of Poland, triggering the Second World War, and changing life for ever.

Eugenie and Xavier are tattooed with a loss of identity; luckily, not with a concentration camp number. Even so, having had to hide their Jewish ancestry they carry the shadow of guilt and shame put onto them through no fault of their own. This remains, locked in the background of their lives.

Being singled out as outcasts, despite secrecy, they have never completely come to terms with this early blight and it remains an integral part of who they are. On the positive side of things, they have evolved from victims into courageous beings and have dealt with life in a positive way.

Hopefully, my recollection of their past will help the next generation to discover who they truly are, and this knowing will spin strong threads, ready to be smoothly woven into the fabric of future lives.

CHILDHOOD REVISITED

As in the Grimm Brothers' story of Hansel and Gretel, remembering is like finding pebbles left on the way.

Memories are colourful wooden blocks, to be assembled and playfully dismantled; later to be reassembled in a new and more exciting way.

JANUARY 2ND, 1934

'I am but a little child: I know not how to go out or come in.'

(King Solomon, I Kings 3:7)

The district of Langfuhr, Dantzig sees the birth of a girl; dropped, so goes the legend, by a stork, flying over a clinic named after this visiting bird. Three or so years later, it also witnesses the birth of the girl's brother.

Both were equally welcomed by their parents, but the girl-child felt threatened by this competitive new arrival. Her beloved nanny had been relocated overnight to care for the new baby. She decided to get rid of this intrusion and placed a pillow over the newborn's head. Fortunately, this was soon discovered and removed without damage to her new brother, who she grew to love very much. He is her companion throughout this story.

Memory: *a bat flies into my brother's nursery, bringing chaos in its wake. It's my first encounter with fear as adults lose their cool.*

Eugenie is addressing the voice of her inner child for guidance along this road. This song reminds her of long walks along endless country lanes, being carried, at times, on the shoulders of a man named Tonton Lucien, who is to play a major role in this story.

Sur la route de Louviers,
Sur la route de Louviers,
Il y avait un cantonnier,
Il y avait un cantonnier,
Et qui cassait,
Et qui cassait,
Des tas d' cailloux,
Des tas d' cailloux,
Et qui cassait des tas d' cailloux
Pour mettre sur l' passag' des roues.

PARIS, 1938

The threatening political climate forced the Poretzky family to move to France. The country of 'liberte, egalite, fraternite' seemed a good enough place, away from the warmongering grumbles of Nazi Germany. Where better than fashionable Paris, so appealing to the pretty redhead, Grounia? Her husband had bought an elegant apartment for them to move into.

They settled to a new life, new language, children, nannie, cook and freedom. Joseph Poretzky continued to demonstrate his timber expertise, purchasing, a forest near Vatan in the Indre region, with a French partner, once the property of diplomat Baron de Lesseps who had developed the Suez Canal.

It offered timber and a hunting ground for indigenous wild boars. It was also home to delicious goats' cheeses dipped in ash and named after their shape as 'Pyramides'.

Life was good.

It was soon clear that Hitler was not ready to stop his megalomania and he marched his soldiers through Europe. The anti-Semitic violence had taken hold and threatened those with Jewish ancestry. Despite what seemed impregnable defences, the Line Maginot crumbled in two days, allowing the German army to enter defenceless

France. The weak Marechal Petain surrendered with a promise that half of the country would remain under French jurisdiction and therefore a Free Zone.

Memory: *Nanny Dita took the children for a walk to the Bois de Boulogne. She was their beloved nanny who was due to return to her country of origin, Dantzig, a promise made to her family should war become imminent. Eugenie was dressed in a navy-blue coat with a white lace collar. On her hands she wore white gloves; on her feet black patent support boots to help her with her left 'flat foot'. They were on their way to the carousel where Eugenie would sit as the proud rider of a magnificently painted wooden horse. The challenge set for her was to throw a ring onto a post while in movement. Eugenie was temporarily transformed from her small self into an Amazonian warrior on horseback.*

The first air raid sirens rang out in Paris and sent the inhabitants of No. 25 rue Raynouard, in the privileged 16th arrondissement, rushing to the cellars. Eugenie, for the first time, experienced uncontrollable fear. Her teeth chattered; her innocence ended. False alarm! No bombs dropped this time, yet fear had lodged, like a worm, under her skin.

She stood in the school playground, leaning against its wired fence. Speech came to her at an early age, but her language was German. She did not understand French and felt isolated, unable to communicate; her inner world and self-confidence shattered.

1939 – 1940

Sensing danger, Joseph Poretzky, having recently passed his driving test, packed his family into his newly acquired Citroen and drove out of Paris towards the Free Zone, leaving all their belongings behind and hoping for an early return. However, it was not to be, and the story of these two children continues during four years of occupation and terror.

Joseph Poretzky sought paid protection, under the wings of a politician named Laval, who would ultimately be remembered for the way he conspired with the Nazi occupation of France while being, effectively, the political head of an unoccupied Vichy France. He seemed to be a strong protective contact for the family.

Under guidance, Joseph aimed to reach the Lot department, in the Free Zone, a sedate underdeveloped part of South West France also known as the Quercy Blanc. The family arrived at a tiny village named Alvignac and booked themselves into two rooms at a local hotel aptly named 'Hotel des Voyageurs'. There, they were to hide and wait for the situation to be resolved, not realising that events would take over. France was to surrender and collaborate with the invaders; but thankfully, not all French people would support this decision. Due to its partial isolation and lack of industry, the Lot region was identified by the Resistance movement as a suitable site for parachutists to land, French volunteers from the UK.

On the journey, little Xavier, not yet two, was afflicted with mumps. The family stopped at a village farm where traditional remedies were given to the boy. An onion poultice was placed on his feet to bring down the fever and he was given macerated prunes to eat and complete the healing.

Eugenie's subconscious was shaped by her observance of these ancient ways.

2

Sur la route de Louviers,
Sur la route de Louviers,
Il y avait un cantonnier,
Il y avait un cantonnier,
Et qui cassait,
Et qui cassait,
Des tas d' cailloux,
Des tas d' cailloux,
Et qui cassait des tas d' cailloux
Pour mettre sur l' passag' des roues.

ON THE WAY 1940 – 1941

Hoping to escape persecution and possible extermination, Joseph Poretzky made his way to Nice, the most distant destination in the Free Zone. He was waiting anxiously for an affidavit from the American government allowing the family to emigrate, and then they would board a boat from the large port of Marseilles. He had considered a clandestine crossing to Spain, but it was too dangerous with small children. The affidavit eventually arrived, but by then no boat could leave France.

Eugenie was gifted a bicycle. She proudly stood for a photo, although she was not yet able to cycle without help.

This was a rare moment of normality.

Alvignac was a small village of around 500 inhabitants in the commune of the Lot region of southwest France. The village itself was not unlike many other French villages except that it had special surroundings. The land in this part of France is referred to as 'Le Quercy Blanc' due to the chalky nature of its soil, in which vines, wheat and maze are grown. It is in the vicinity of Rocamadour, a famous pilgrimage destination that would have a profound effect on Eugenie.

L'Hotel du Chateau was a grand residence; in front of its boundary wall grew a large Magnolia tree with large smooth leaves and enormously luxurious, white, waxy flowers; a sight of utter fascination for this small child. (On returning to that spot as an adult, she discovered that the tree was still there but not very tall.)

Eugenie's parents hired the baker's daughter to look after her. The ensuing walks created a close connection to the earth for the city-reared child, forming memories she would never forget, like being eye-to-eye with a hare whilst spending a penny under bright yellow broom; feeling the wind on her cheeks as it swept over les 'Causses'; exploring the underworld grotto at Le Gouffre de Padirac, where gleaming stalactites hung from high vaulted rocks, dripping water from the source of a deep lake. This was an underground space of magic where one was dwarfed by the magnitude of nature's beauty; a place where fairies gathered.

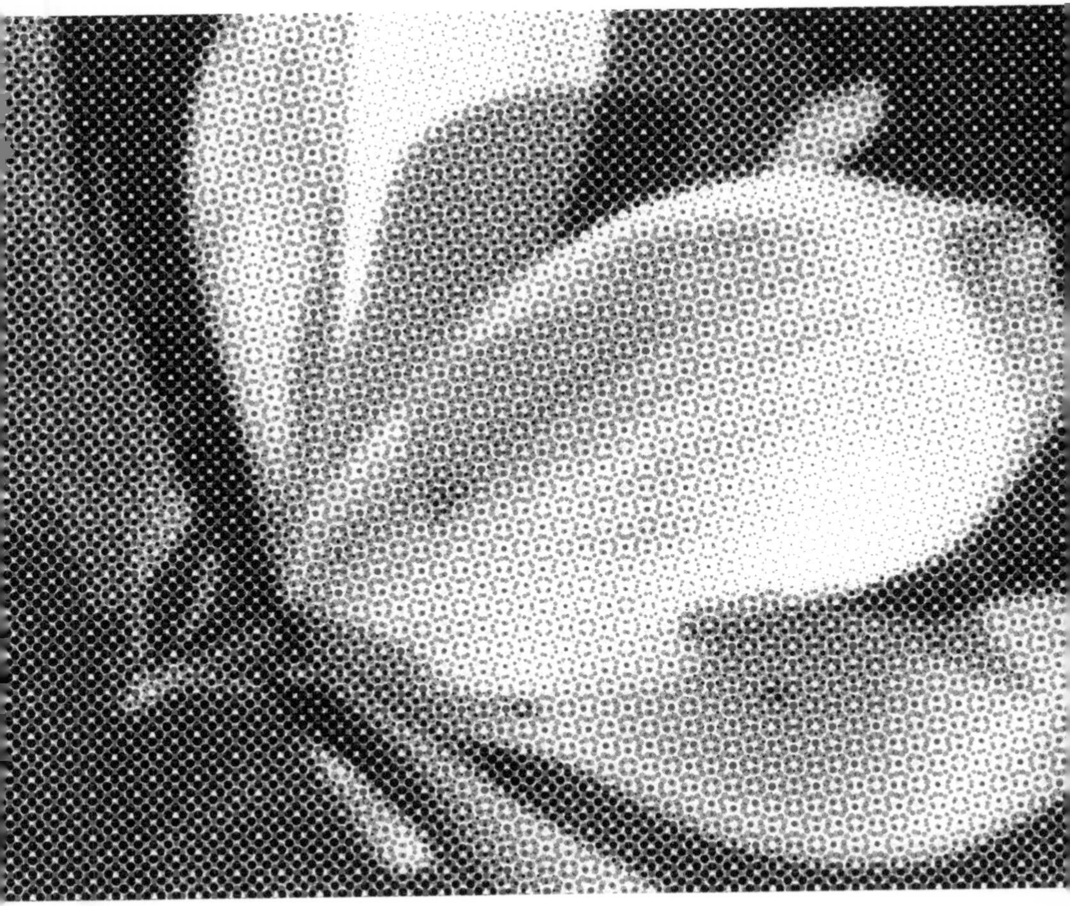

These experiences opened a propensity of sympathy for 'small folks'; fairies, goblins, nature spirits and the like. For Eugenie the connection was put in place, never to change. On special days a large grey aluminium bucket would be filled with hot water. These were the bathing rituals. Both children were plunged into the welcome warmth of the water and scrubbed. For the Poretzky family, life had changed beyond belief. Wallpapered, seedy rooms, cold uncertainty . . . They had to wait out their situation, trusting in an uncertain future. False identity documents had been provided and, hiding behind a new identity, they now responded to the shortened surname of 'Poret', a more Gallic-sounding presence.

ROCAMADOUR

Rocamadour, an unusual place, lay in the vicinity of Alvignac. Somehow, Eugenie was taken there. An impressionable young girl, this visit had an immense impact on her, ultimately shaping her spirit for life.

It had been a place of pilgrimage since the early Middle Ages. According to history, Rocamadour was named after the founder of an ancient sanctuary, Saint Amator, associated with the Biblical Zacheus, the tax collector of Jericho mentioned in Luke 19:1-10, and the husband of St. Veronica, who wiped Jesus' face on the way to Calvary. Driven out of Palestine by persecution, St. Amadour and Veronica embarked on a frail skiff and, guided by an angel, came to a pagan shrine dedicated to the Earth Mother Goddess, which St. Amadour replaced with a Black Virgin. Worship of the Mother Goddess was very extensive throughout the Roman Empire; the most popular in France being Cybele and Isis. Pilgrims were drawn to the site by the Miracles of Our Lady of Rocamadour, the Black Virgin.

Inside her chapel was an air of serenity. From the roof hung a 6th-century bell, which miraculously rang of its own accord to warn sailors of storms and to foretell miracles.

Above the altar, the Black Virgin, 66 centimetres high and carved from walnut, rested in an alcove. According to the guidebooks the statue dates back to the 9th century AD.

The walls were decorated with ex-votos, left by those cured or saved through Black Virgin's intervention, the protector of small children. A fact which takes on a deeper meaning as this story evolves.

Eugenie was transfixed by her image and by the energy emanating from this small carving. She carried away with her a devotional impulse that was to endure. She created shrines inside hollow trees with pictures and other small pieces that seemed relevant to her creativity. She projected towards the altar some of the magic found in the natural cave of Padirac and she ran riot with local children, waving a wooden stick as a sword, impersonating medieval knights. Eugenie's imaginative, romantic nature had found a perfect outlet for expression, which was violently interrupted after witnessing the local hotel proprietor cutting off the head of a chicken, which, despite being headless, continued to fly.

Eugenie was walking in a field of long grasses when, out of nowhere, a solitary plane appeared, flying low. She could see the black German cross on its wings. Terrified, she started running, running, falling, as it flew away over her, even though the pilot might have been waving.

Sur la route de Louviers,
Sur la route de Louviers,
Il y avait un cantonnier,
Il y avait un cantonnier,
Et qui cassait,
Et qui cassait,
Des tas d' cailloux,
Des tas d' cailloux,
Et qui cassait des tas d' cailloux
Pour mettre sur l' passag' des roues.

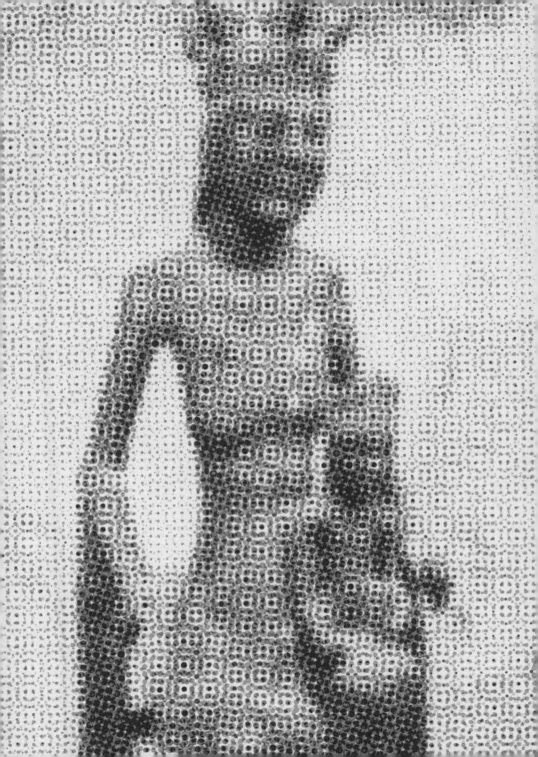

Things became worse for the family. The small-minded, post office woman reported to the Gestapo the presence in the village of foreign Jews. By then, the so-called Free Zone had been eroded and France now followed Nazi policies. One day, men dressed in dark leather arrived with a truck and picked up the Poretzky family to be transported to the transit camp of Septfonds, in the Tarn-et-Garonne department in the Midi-Pyrénées region in southern France. This camp, was originally set up to lodge refugees from the Spanish uprising and was now used to keep Jews in transit before deporting them to concentration-death camps.

The facilities there were minimal and depressing.

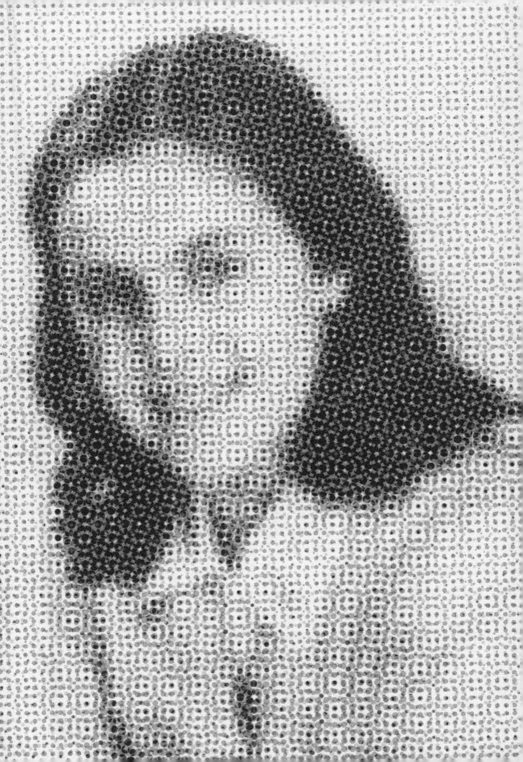

Grunia's friend, Mme. Robillard, from the city of Lille in Northern France, the wife of the local choirmaster, had a Jewish lover. Following after him and his attempt to hide, she found herself in Alvignac, and became a compassionate friend of hers. She taught Grunia the craft of knitting, and together they would spend long hours creating various items of clothing from the harsh local spun wool, impossibly itchy to the skin. But when it became cold, there was little protestation! Socks were essential. Their companionship was a welcome distraction from the fear and helplessness. In the months that followed, Madame Robillard used to creep, at dusk, to the edge of the camp's barbed-wired fence in the hope of finding a hole and a way to rescue Xavier from an unknown and threatening future, from the hands of his mother. It was not to be. At this stage, Eugenie's recollection was wiped out; amnesia may have been induced by fear. Old men lying on the floor and people stranded next to each other are the only shadow memories from this sad episode. The place was dirty and full of desperate people.

The next memory frame recalls a wooden bench in a train compartment. Her father was not there. Dirty tears smudged her cheeks. The train had stopped to fill the engine with water. On the platform, a young man was running, waving a piece of paper. He gave it to the guard in charge. The doors opened and she was helped out over steep steps, followed by her mother holding Xavier in her arms. At the far end of the platform stood their father. The doors closed and the train departed. Faces pressed against the windows of the moving compartments seemed to be shouting and knocking on the glass panes with their fists.

A young man aged 15, named Jackie Latscha, carried a letter written by his father, Jean Latscha, who was, by then, an important civil servant. In February, 1942, he was named General Secretary of the Pyrenees Orientales. He was also in charge of the selection of Jews arrested in Southern France and sent to extermination camps. As a 'Gaullist' he joined the Resistance movement, specialising in facilitating escapees from France.

He had met Joseph at an earlier date when staying in the Lot. They became friends and Joseph helped Jean financially with his divorce settlement. Money, which was returned after the war.

Colchiques dans les prés
Fleurissent, fleurissent
Colchiques dans les prés
C'est la fin de l'été
La feuille d'automne
Emportée par le vent
En rondes monotones
Tombant, tourbillonnant

The Poretzky family had been saved. Joseph had to spend a while in another camp from where he eventually escaped and managed to rejoin his wife and children.

Eugenie feels this miracle is a blessing of the Black Virgin of Rocamadour.

She carries to this day the vision of those petrified faces behind the windows of the departing train.

Sur la route de Louviers,
Sur la route de Louviers,
Il y avait un cantonnier,
Il y avait un cantonnier,
Et qui cassait,
Et qui cassait,
Des tas d' cailloux,
Des tas d' cailloux,
Et qui cassait des tas d' cailloux
Pour mettre sur l' passag' des roues.

1943 – 1944

The Poretzky family found themselves in the village of Lestrade in the department of the Puy-de-Dome area of the Auvergne-Central France. Once again, they sought refuge in a small hotel. They huddled together in one room where, in the winter months, the water froze at night in the washing bowl. The toilet facilities were outdoors, amounting to a hole in the ground. They were not the only refugees in hiding. A family friend Igor Siskind shared the lodgings. He was Xavier's godfather, having somehow found his way to Lestrade. The hotel kitchen was the warmest place in the house. All the guests met there for meals.

By the stove sat the ancient grandmother, dressed in black from head to toe. To keep her occupied she was given wool remnants to knit, day after day, an endless, narrow scarf. Eugenie eventually discovered that, as in the myth of Penelope, the knitting was undone at night, ready to be resumed the following day. Eugenie found it hypnotic.

Opposite the hotel, on a piece of wasteland, was parked the rusty remains of an abandoned truck. Xavier delighted in turning the wheel, being the driver, making loud pretend engine noises. His sister sat, bored, watching.

Not long after, Eugenie was sent to a convent. Her parents may have wanted to protect her as well as give her an education. At night, as she lay in her bed in the crowded dormitory, a nun would come turn off the lights. Eugenie peeped behind a curtain and saw her shaven head. Was this a nightmare?

Later, during communion in church, she did not know what to do and followed the other children, pulling out her tongue to receive the host before being guided to confession. She quickly invented some sins and was told to say a few 'Hail Mary's' for contrition. This was no problem, for SHE was a nice lady; Mary would certainly forgive her lies.

Six o'clock in the morning; it was mass time, come rain or shine. There was snow on the ground. Eugenie had lost one of her wooden clogs and walked, barefoot, to the church.

Her parents later had to fetch her. She had a high fever and was diagnosed with pleurisy by a local doctor. He cured her with sulfonamides, before antibiotics had been invented. It turned out later that he was an active member of the Maquis, or French Resistance. Eugenie was spared a return to the convent.

A chimney fire at the hotel consumed her with fear. She ran outside into the night with nothing on but her nightclothes. There was snow on the ground. It took a while before she was found and sheltered back inside.

The Germans were driving through the village. Joseph was a courageous man. He took his children by their hands and walked calmly past a soldier, who greeted the pretty children in a friendly manner. He walked towards a forest in close vicinity, walking deeper and deeper into the woods, collecting mushrooms, staying still, out of sight. In the distance, the 'hack hack' sound of the tommy guns reached their ears. The Resistance was blocking the road and was being fired at. The same brave doctor attempted to save desperately wounded young French boys. The bullets used by the German army exploded internally, causing irreparable damage to their bodies.

For the nine months before D-Day, Xavier and Eugenie were once more separated from their parents. It had become more and more dangerous.

They were handed for 'safe keeping' to Lucien Grant and his family, consisting of two boys and his wife Suzanne. Lucien had left Paris and was living now in the presbytery of La Selle les Bains, a tiny hamlet.

He had been one of the administrators at the camp of Drancy outside Paris. From there, Jews were rounded up and selected to be sent to extermination camps. He took us into his care, probably as insurance in case the Germans lost the war.

One of Lucien's unmistakable features was that he only had one arm, 'un manchot', the other being a stump.

When the time came for retribution, camp survivors had him arrested and, despite my child-like testimony requested by his defence, Lucien was condemned to 12 years' imprisonment in Algeria.

Tonton Lucien was very kind to Eugenie and her younger brother. He might have liked to have had a daughter of his own.

Eugenie was sent to the local convent school. The teaching nun, after tapping her itchy coif, regularly fell asleep. All the children would run out in the yard only to slip back when she rubbed her eyes and stopped snoring. So much for effective education!

Eugenie had fun climbing trees with the boys, looking at pale blue eggs in birds' nests, learning to 'tickle' trouts in the local stream; the slow ones, resting under the weeds by the verges, could be caught with bare hands if you were lucky.

Behind a tall brick wall by the side of the presbytery was an ancient cemetery. It was said that bones stuck out of its abandoned graves. Despite a frisson curiosity, Eugenie never ventured to check. The whole place, in fact, was eerie. That same wall was also used by the boys, including small Xavier, to pee against to see who could aim highest. One day, a uniformed postman, approached along the path leading to the house, which sent Eugenie running and screaming in deep panic. She believed herself and her brother to be in danger, but little Xavier unaware continued to walk long distances in the winter snow to collect milk from the farm.

For him it was all an adventure.

3

Sur la route de Louviers,
Sur la route de Louviers,
Il y avait un cantonnier,
Il y avait un cantonnier,
Et qui cassait,
Et qui cassait,
Des tas d' cailloux,
Des tas d' cailloux,
Et qui cassait des tas d' cailloux
Pour mettre sur l' passag' des roues.

(*Sur la route de Louviers* – An historical French
song dating from around 1820)

1945

After 9 months apart, Grunia and Joseph Poretzky found the separation from their children too much to bear. They took them back to Lestrade. By then, the Germans were losing the war, but not before the family had witnessed a famous war crime, remembered in French history.

Oradour-sur-Glane.

As a punishment for the killing of a German officer by the 'Maquis', soldiers surrounded the village, locked the inhabitants in the church and set fire to it. All perished, except for one boy who witnessed the event from the fields where he was hiding. Trucks carrying those soldiers drove through Lestrade in front of our eyes. It was said they were Ukrainian. Germans chose them to perform their worst atrocities.

The sky was dark with planes and the sound deafening. Eugenie ran out of the outdoor toilet without even lifting her knickers. American planes were relentless, day after day, bombing the nearby town of Clermont-Ferrand, the centre of the Michelin Tyre industry.

It was soon over.

Memories from the intervening months are blurred. Life did return to some sort of sanity.

PROLOGUE

So many fragments to pick up! This family had survived, despite the odds. Maybe the gracious Lady of Rocamadour had played a part in the events.

The family eventually returned to Paris, damaged but alive, to the place they had left over four years previously. On many levels, the harm was still felt in their adult lives. Recent research shows that fear at an early age is imprinted on the brain cortex. Remaining aware of this mark is the only homeopathy available to persons affected by unjust violence and discrimination. Eugenie and Xavier, amongst them, are sharing their childhood memories partly to help unwind the tangles left in their psyche.

Their story, witnessed through children's eyes, must stop here. Childhood is most precious, even when persecuted. May it be read with this in mind!

Eugenie and Xavier are voicing the tale. It is dedicated to their children and grandchildren in the hope that they will live a peaceful and fulfilling life.

With gratitude to Grunia and Joseph, our parents, who always did the best they knew how. Also for Xavier, beloved brother (1937–2017).

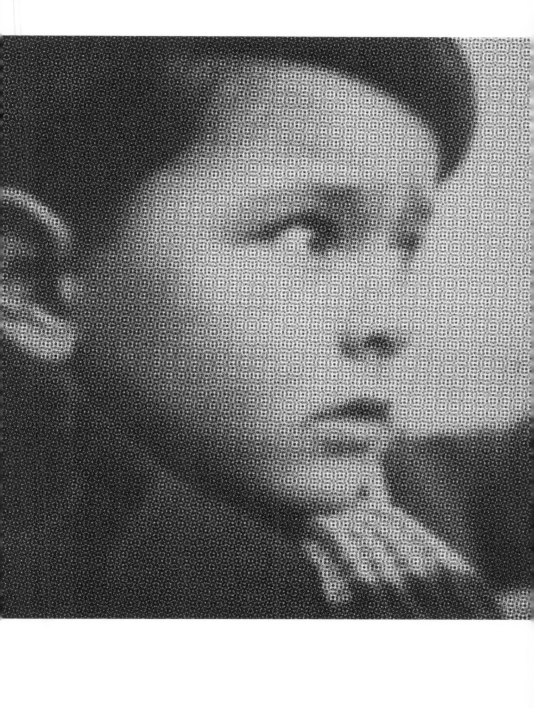

'It is, in fact, quite likely that the invincible sadness that sometimes overwhelms children is born precisely from their awareness that they are incapable of magic. Whatever we can achieve through merit and effort, cannot make us truly happy. Only magic can do that.'

Giorgio Agamben

Lightning Source UK Ltd.
Milton Keynes UK
UKHW040701310720
367475UK00001B/47